First Lessons® Clarinet

by Jeremy Viner

Online Audio www.melbay.com/30007BCDEB

Audio Contents

1 2 3 4 5 6 7 8 9 0

Visit us on the Web at www.melbay.com — E-mail us at email@melbay.com.

Introduction

This book is designed to teach both children and adults beginning technique on the clarinet along with basic music reading skills. Exercises are tailored to assist in gradually integrating newly learned techniques. The lessons that follow include basic clarinet technique, music reading skills, care and maintenance, and musical techniques like articulation and dynamics. There are 43 exercises and melodies to help explore the techniques learned in the lessons. These include classical melodies from composers like Bach, Beethoven, Mozart, and Dukas. The companion audio recording has examples of all 43 exercises and melodies as played on clarinet with piano accompaniment.

Table of Contents

The Clarinet, Mouthpiece, and Reed

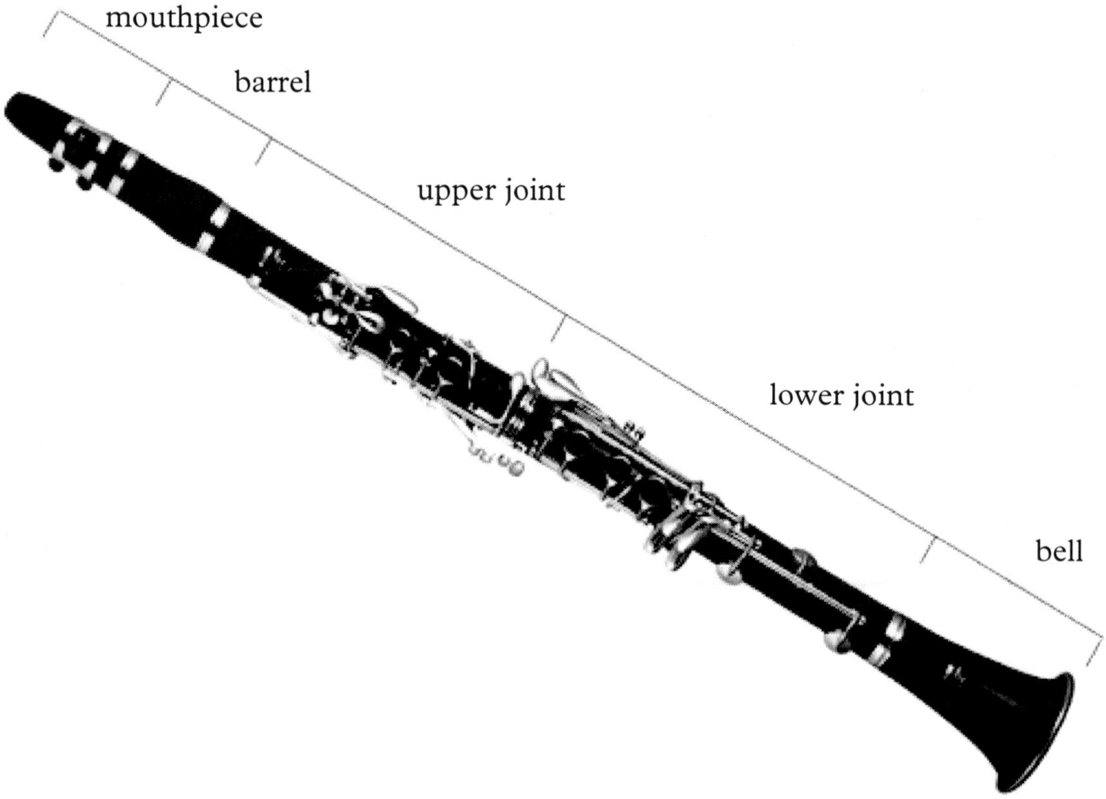

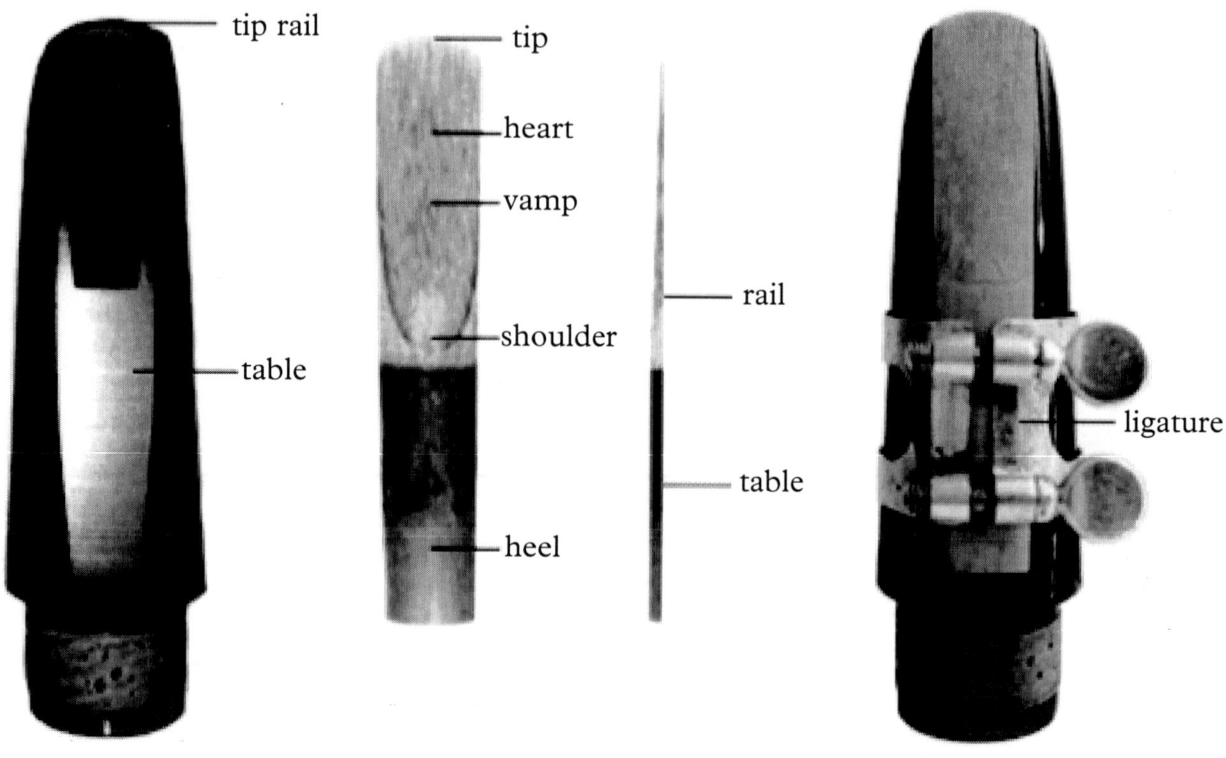

The reed should be secured to the table of the mouthpiece with a ligature. Only tighten the ligature enough so that the reed stays in place. The tip of the reed should line up with the tip of the mouthpiece to create a good seal. Make sure the ligature's screw(s) are facing right and that it is secured to the reed at the heel. The top of the ligature should not go above the heel.

Assembling and Holding the Clarinet

Make sure to reference the opposite page to identify the different parts of the clarinet.

Assembling the Clarinet

- First, take out a reed that you can keep in your mouth while putting the instrument together so that it will be ready to play when you are finished.

- Take the upper joint in your right hand and the lower joint in your left hand. On the upper joint, press down the key that's over the second hole with your right thumb. This should lift the bridge key on the upper joint. Holding down this key with your right thumb, screw the upper joint into the lower joint and line up the bridge keys. The thumb rest on the back should also be in line with the thumb keys on the upper joint. If there is a lot a of resistance while trying to assemble any of these pieces you can apply a little cork grease to the corks at the ends of the joints and mouthpiece.

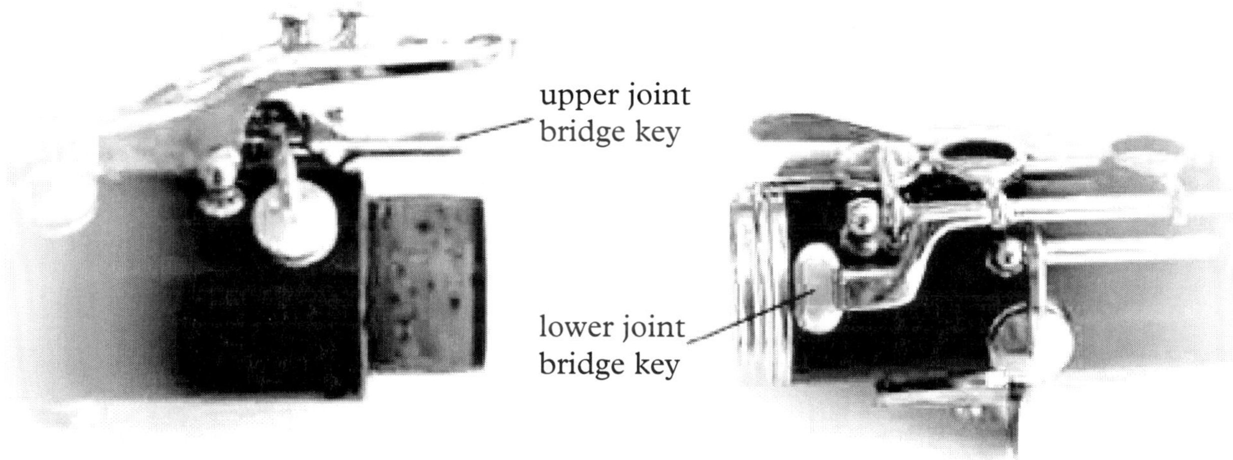

- Attach the bell to the lower joint; then attach the barrel to the upper joint.

- Place down your clarinet (always place down the clarinet with keys facing up) and assemble your mouthpiece. Take the reed you've been preparing and secure it to the mouthpiece. Refer to the bottom of the opposite page to to ensure proper reed placement.

- Attach the mouthpiece to the barrel. The reed should be lined up with the left hand thumb keys and right hand thumb rest.

Holding the Clarinet

- Place your right thumb under the thumb rest on the lower joint. Almost all of your support comes from the right thumb so avoid applying more pressure than is needed to seal the keys.

- Cover the 3 holes on the upper joint with the pads of your left fingers. Your fingers should slightly curve around the upper joint. Cover the hole on the back of the upper joint with your left thumb.

- Cover the three holes on the lower joint with the pads of your right fingers. Your fingers should slightly curve around the lower joint.

The Clarinet Embouchure

The **clarinet embouchure** is the shape of your mouth in relation to the clarinet mouthpiece. There are a few steps to creating the proper clarinet embouchure. As the embouchure makes use of your facial muscles it must be exercised correctly in order to develop strength.

Steps To Creating A Proper Embouchure

1. Put your lips together tightly.
2. Stretch your lower lip against your bottom teeth.
3. Draw your jaw enough to part your lips.
4. Insert the mouthpiece in the center of your mouth and rest the tip of the reed on your bottom lip.
5. Push the mouthpiece into your mouth so that the reed pushes your bottom lip over your bottom teeth.
6. Rest your upper teeth on top of the mouthpiece. Bring your upper lip down on top of the mouthpiece.
7. Shape your mouth as if you are saying "who". This should create the proper seal.

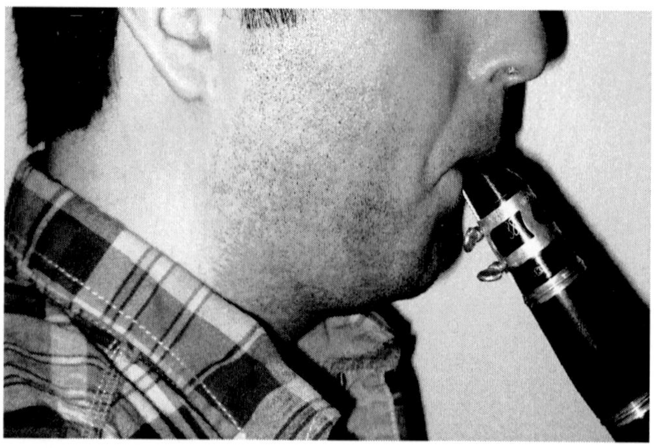

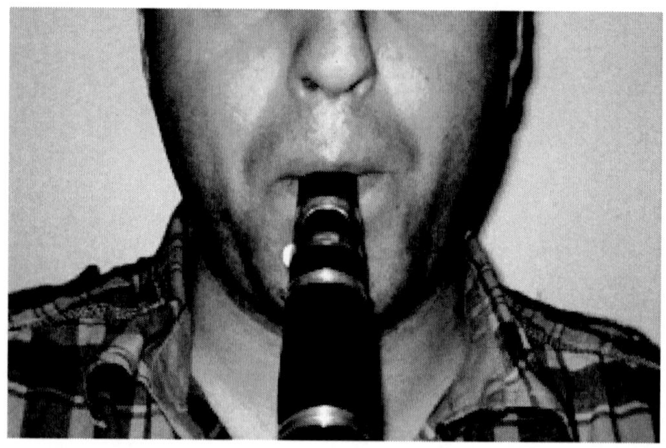

Common Embouchure Problems

1. Puffing your cheeks.
2. Not placing your top teeth on the mouthpiece.
3. Bunching up the muscles in your chin... the chin should be flat and pointed downward.
4. Holding the instrument to far away from you creating too wide of an angle where the mouthpiece enters.

You can avoid soreness and build the strength of your embouchure muscles by playing long tones. Avoid practicing for excessive amounts of time. You should extend your practice time gradually. Make sure you practice your embouchure in a mirror so that you can see if there are any problems.

Posture and Breathing

Correct **posture** will have a significant effect on your breathing, technique, stamina, and sound on the clarinet. Proper posture will also help ensure against fatigue and serious injuries like carpal tunnel.

A Proper Seated Posture

1. Sit up straight with both feet flat on the floor. Sit toward the front of the chair.
2. Keep your head straight. Do not bend your neck and reach for the mouthpiece. Rather, keep your head level and relaxed and bring the mouthpiece to your mouth.

Make sure you don't place the music stand too low. You don't want to have to bend your neck down in order to see the music - this will inhibit your ability to breath properly.

Breathing

Control over your breathing is the most important factor of your overall musicianship as a clarinetist. The use of your air affects every aspect of playing the clarinet - dynamics, intonation, articulation, and other techniques that we'll be looking at in this book. There are a few important concepts about breathing that should be addressed.

When breathing in, your abdominal area should expand along with the chest, back, and ribcage. It is very important that you do not raise your shoulders when inhaling. Make sure you keep your body relaxed while breathing but do not slouch. Your lung capacity and your ability to draw in a large amount of air in a short amount of time can be improved with training. When breathing while playing clarinet, keep the reed on the bottom lip and breath in from the corners of your mouth. The goal is to change your embouchure as little as possible while breathing in so you are ready to play the next phrase as soon as you have finished taking your breath.

Clarinet Care & Maintenance

Maintaining your clarinet is very important to ensure optimal playing conditions. Here is a list of routine maintenance for your clarinet.

1. Always take your clarinet apart and put it away properly when finished playing. Reference *Assembling the Clarinet* to make sure you are doing this properly.
2. Grease your corks regularly so that you don't put too much pressure on the joints while assembling and disassembling the clarinet.
3. Make sure you keep your hands in the correct position while holding the clarinet to avoid bending any of the keys.
4. During disassembly, swab out out each section of the clarinet individually. You can repeat the swabbing process multiple times to ensure you have got out all of the moisture. This is particularly important for wooden clarinets. Also make sure you wipe any excess moisture from the tenons.
5. You can wipe down the outside of the clarinet with a dry, soft cloth to remove dust and excess moisture.
6. A mouthpiece saver can be used to cushion the top teeth on the mouthpiece and to help prevent damage to the mouthpiece.
7. Use a mouthpiece cap to avoid damaging the tip of the mouthpiece.

If you have a wooden clarinet then you will need to apply bore oil a few times every year. I would suggest doing this when the seasons change as a good way to make sure the wood is being treated consistently enough. You should ask a clarinet technician or instructor for advice regarding oiling your clarinet.

Reed Care

The following list should help you get the most out of your reeds and prevent damaging them.

1. Make sure you hold reeds at the heel end when handling them. Touching reads at the tip will cause build-up of oil and grime.
2. Cover the reed and mouthpiece with a mouthpiece cap when resting for extended periods of time. Make sure you do not push the mouthpiece cap down too far though as it may damage the tip of the reed.
3. Break in reeds by using them for a few minutes each day - this will help extend the life of the reed. Rotate your reeds three or four at a time if possible.
4. Avoid eating and drinking anything but water while practicing.
5. Do not handle your reeds with dirty hands.
6. Store your reeds in a reed case to avoid damaging them.

Clarinet Tablature

Here is a visual aid to help in understanding how the clarinet fingerings in this book are represented. The clarinet tablature used is a full graphic representation of the keys on the clarinet. The tablature is laid out as though you were facing the instrument. The left hand fingerings are represented on the top half of the tablature while the bottom half represents right hand fingerings. In the first few lessons of this book you'll be learning fingerings for new notes. Reference this page to see which fingers should be used to attain the correct fingering. Any keys that are filled in (black) should be pressed/covered. Keys that are not filled in (as they appear below) should not be pressed/covered.

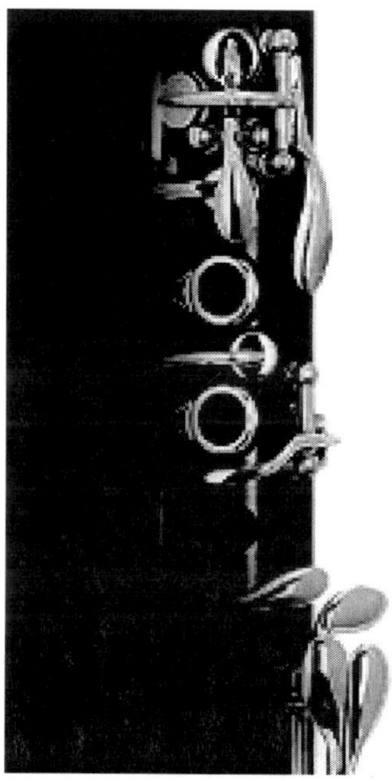

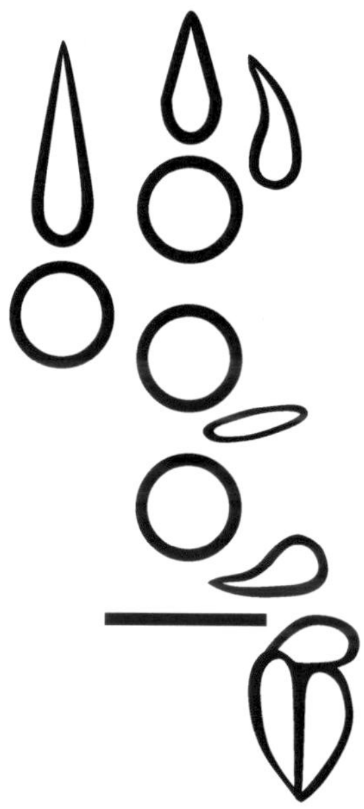

LEFT HAND

The three circles on the right correspond to where your left index, middle, and ring fingers rest. The third hole does not have a metal key above it.

The two keys on the left of the tab indicate the keys on the back of the clarinet. These are played with your left thumb.

The key above the three circles represents the "A" key and is played with the left index finger. The key immediately to the right of the "A" key is the "G-sharp" key and is played with the lower left index finger/left palm.

The small key between the second and third finger is for more advanced fingerings and won't be used in this book.

The key below the third finger and the three keys to its right are played by the left pinky.

RIGHT HAND

The three circles on the right correspond to where your right index, middle, and ring fingers rest.

The four keys to the left correspond to the four side keys on the clarinet. These are played with the side of the right index finger.

The small key between the second and third finger is for more advanced fingerings and won't be used in this book.

The four keys at the bottom of the diagram are played with the right pinky.

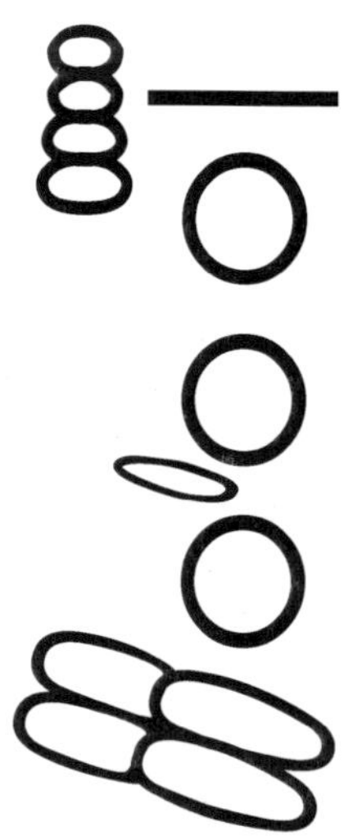

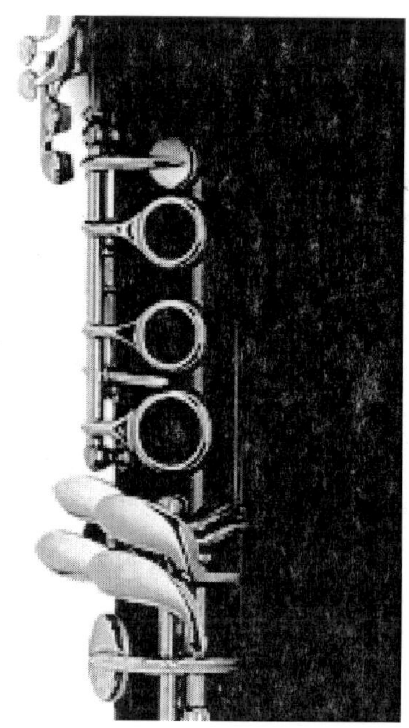

Music Reading Fundamentals

The Staff, Treble Clef, and Measures

The staff is made up of **5 lines** with **4 spaces** between them:

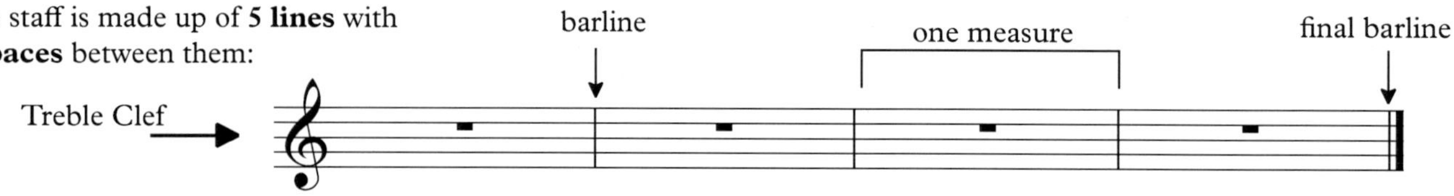

Notes on the Lines

Every **G**ood **B**oy **D**oes **F**ine:

Notes on the Spaces

FACE:

4/4 Time Signature and Note Lengths

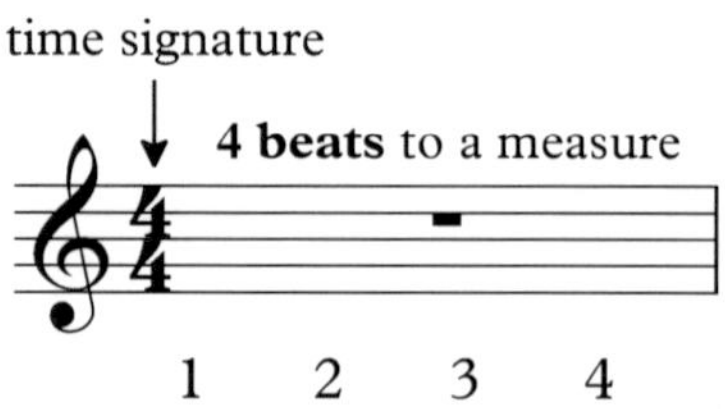

Whole Note = 4 beats

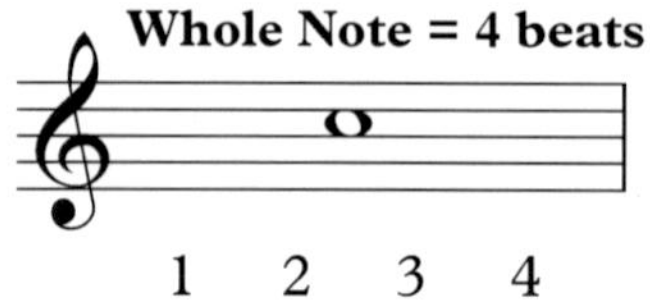

Half Note = 2 beats

Quarter Note = 1 beat

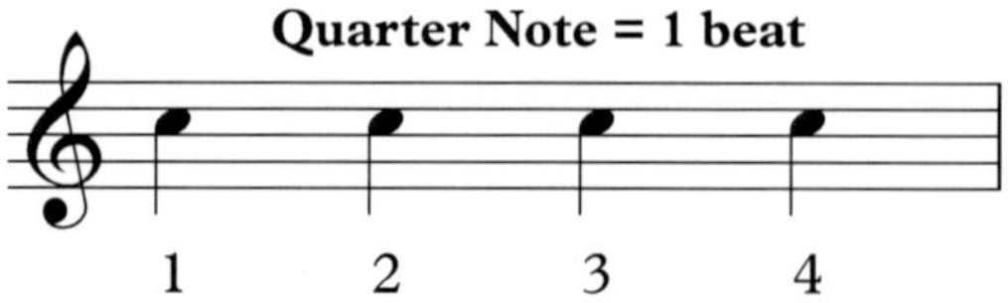

Eighth Note = 1/2 beat

Learning New Notes, Developing Your Sound and Embouchure

The first few lessons will teach you how to play specific notes on the clarinet. The fingerings are coupled with the note as it's seen on the staff as a whole note. When learning these fingerings, play each note for a full breath. To help develop your sound and embouchure try playing each new note in the following ways: 1) from soft to loud in one breath; 2) from loud to soft in one breath; 3) from soft to loud and back to soft in one breath.

Tonguing

To start each new note, lightly touch the tip of the reed with the tip of your tongue. The tongue will prevent the reed from vibrating, resulting in no sound. When you release your tongue from the reed the note should sound. All notes should be tongued at the beginning unless notated otherwise (something we will get into in **Lesson 15**). The tongue should move quickly and lightly between notes as if you're saying the syllable "**tu**".

Lesson 1

First Notes: C, D, and E

Track 1 **Exercise 1-1**

(breath mark)

Track 2 **Exercise 1-2**

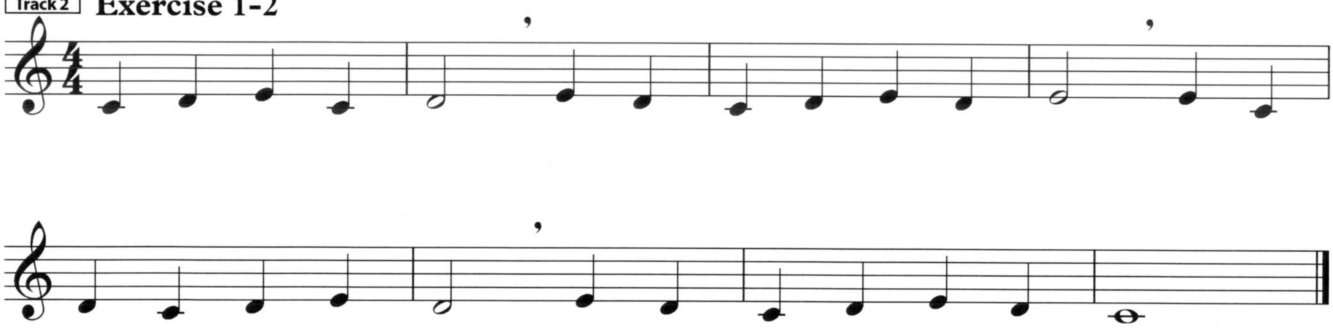

Track 3 **Mary Had A Little Lamb**

Track 4 **Hot Cross Buns**

Lesson 2

New Notes: F, G, and A

F

(no fingers down)

G

(key above first tone hole played with the index finger)

A

Track 5 **Exercise 2-1**

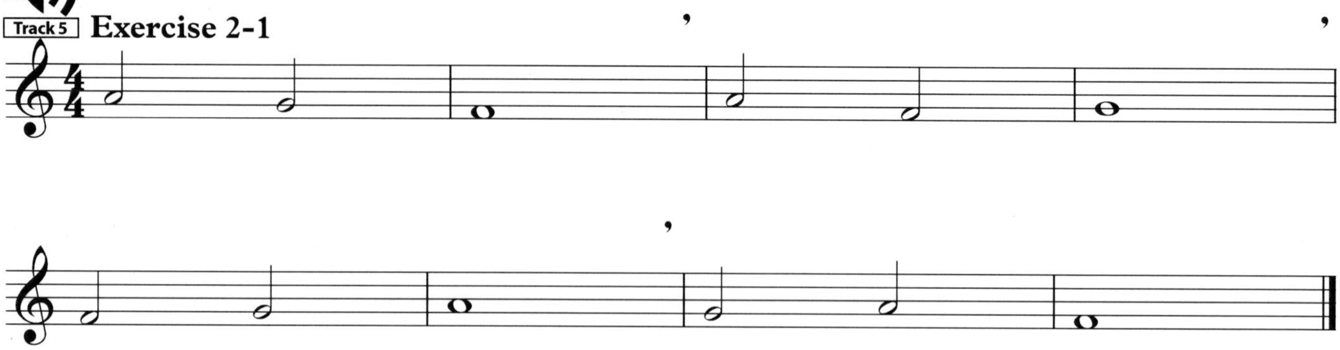

Track 6 **Exercise 2-2**

Track 7 **Exercise 2-3**

Track 8 **Exercise 2-4**

Lesson 3

Sharps and Flats (Accidentals)

Accidentals carry through the measure. In this example the **F#** is carried through to the last note of the first measure. Accidentals do not carry over to the next measure so another accidental is needed in the second measure to make the **F** sharp again.

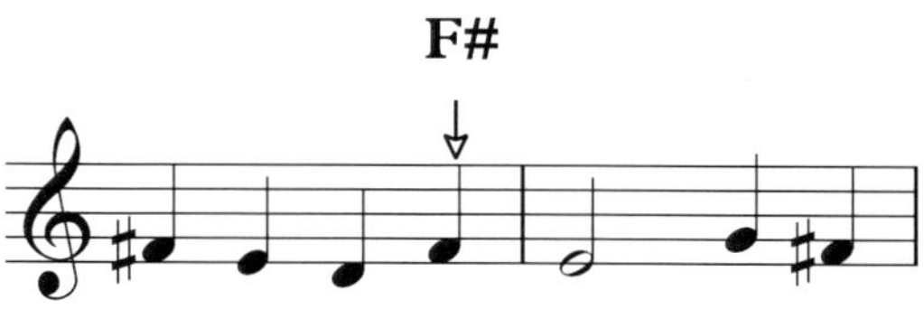

F# or Gb

G# or Ab

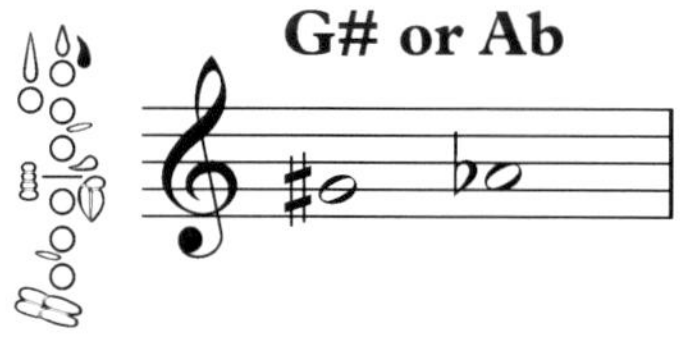

A# or Bb

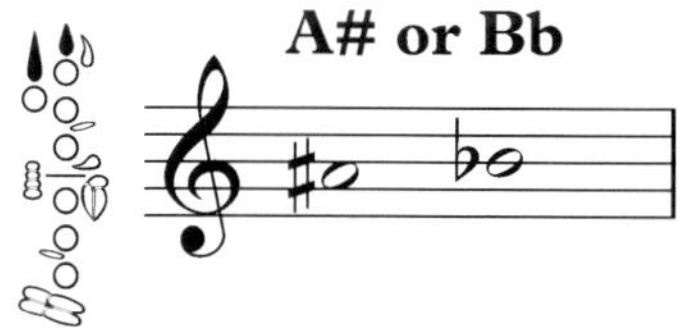

Track 9 **Exercise 3-1**

Track 10 **Exercise 3-2**

Track 11 **Exercise 3-3**

Lesson 4

Ledger Lines and The Chalumeau Register

Ledger lines are used to aid in reading notes that go below or above the staff.

The **chalumeau register** is the lower range of the clarinet. We've already learned half of the chalumeau register. The chalumeau register consists of all the notes from the **Bb** we learned in **Lesson 3** to the lowest note on the clarinet - the **low E**.

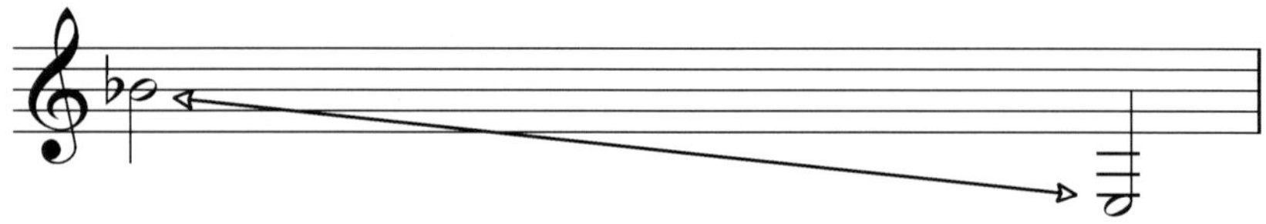

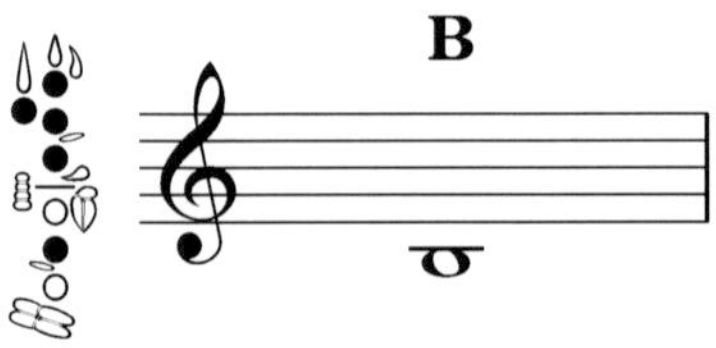

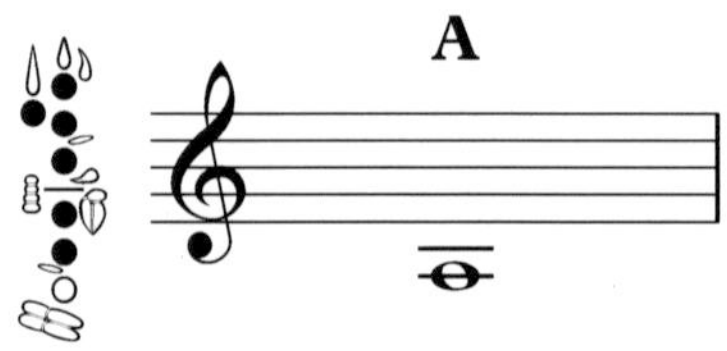

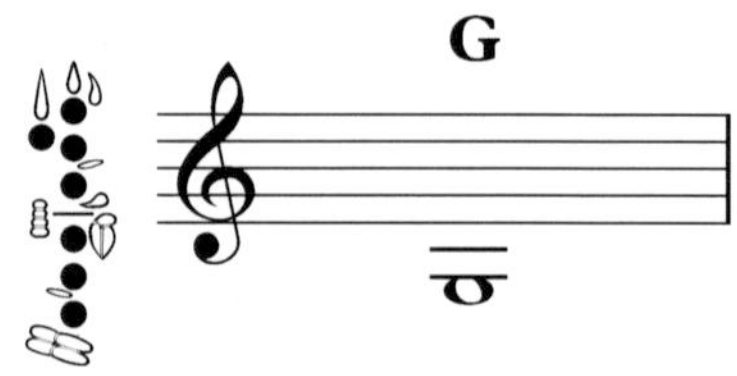

Track 12 **Exercise 4-1**

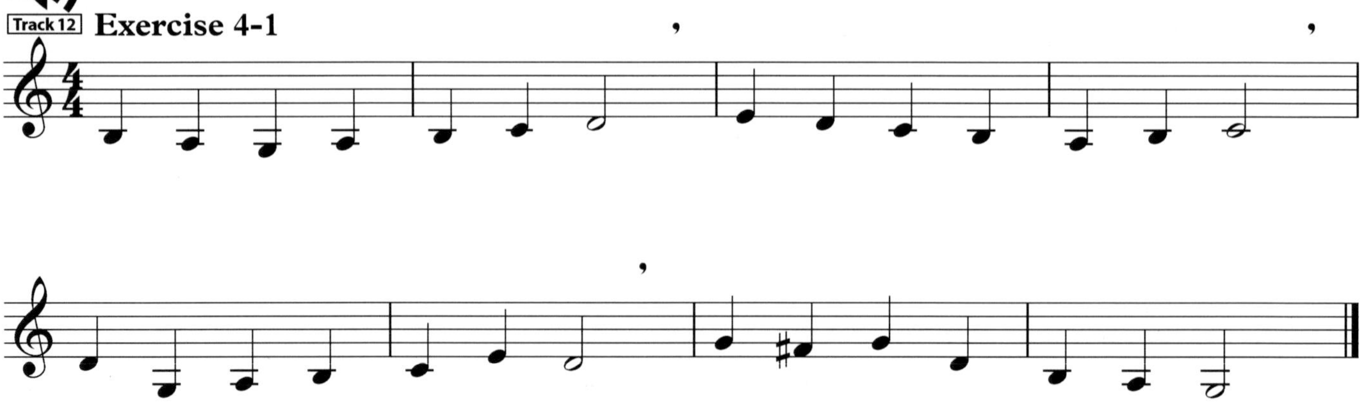

Track 13 **Exercise 4-2**

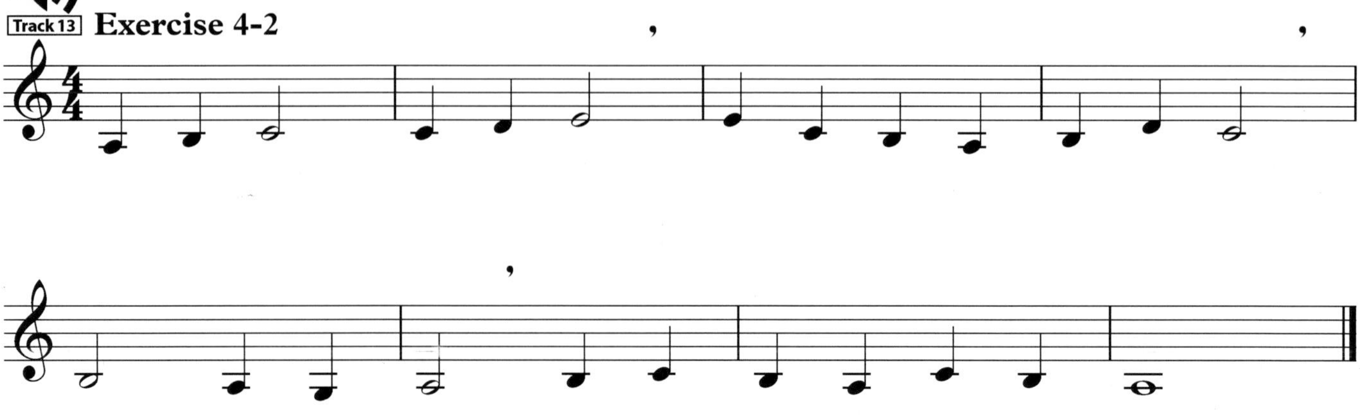

Lesson 5

Rests

A **whole** rest is **4** beats.

A **half** rest is **2** beats.

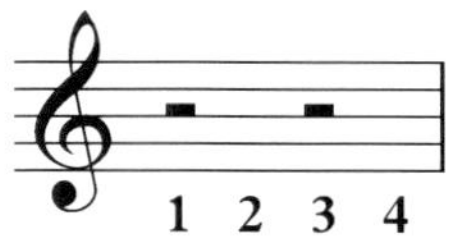

A **quarter** rest is **1** beat.

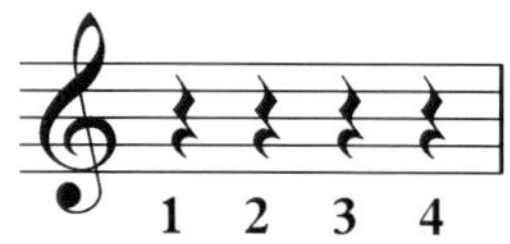

There are two **eighth** rests per beat.

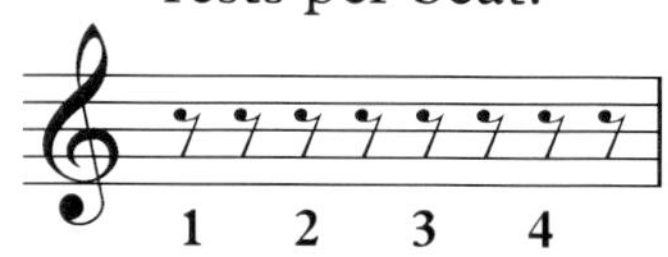

F

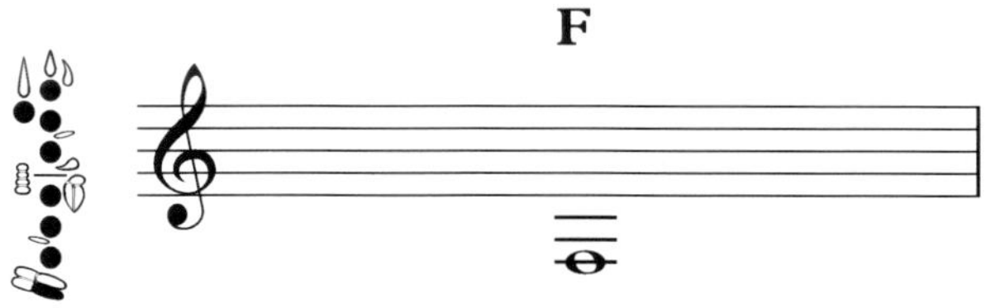

E

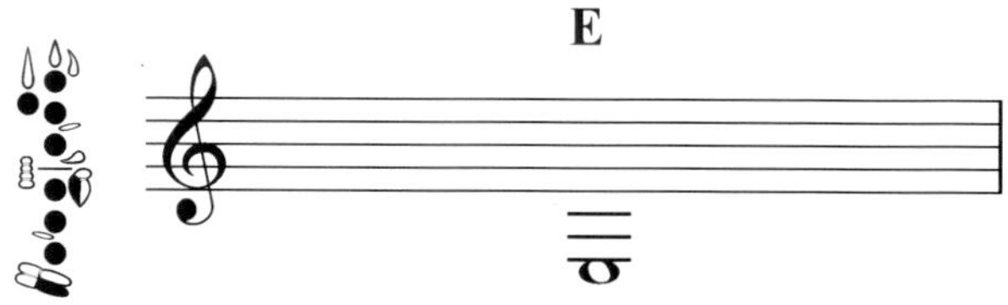

Track 14 **Rest in Show**

Track 15 **Rest Assured**

Lesson 6

Ties

A **tie** indicates that a note is to be held to another note. Ties are used to hold notes over from one measure to the next. They can also be used within a measure. **Accidentals** carry over to the next measure **only if** the note is tied.

D# or Eb

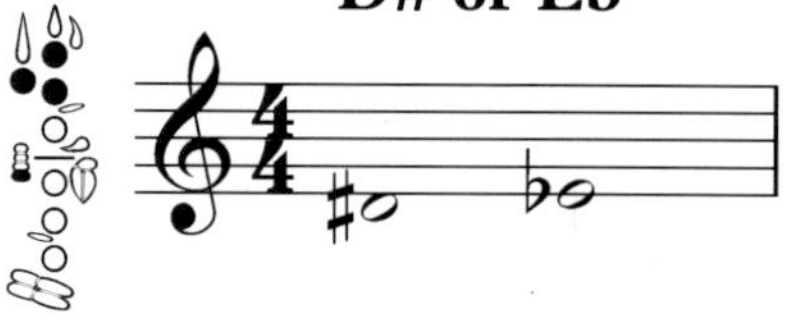

C# or Db

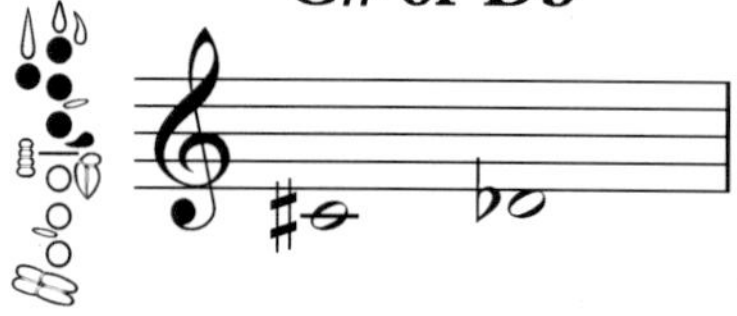

A# or Bb

Track 16 **Tie Me Over**

Track 17 **Tied Down**

Lesson 7

More Accidentals

Here are the last two notes of the **chalumeau** register. Remember accidentals **do** carry over to the next measure **only if** the note is **tied**.

G# or Ab

F# or Gb

Track 18 **Holding On**

Track 19 **Over the Bar**

Lesson 8

New Notes: B, C and Bridging the Octave

B

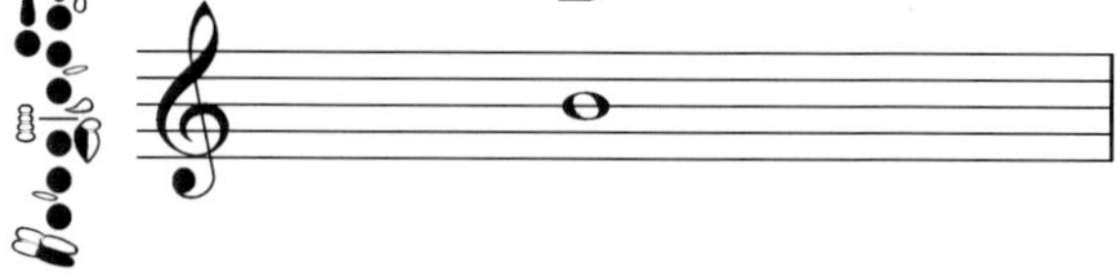

C

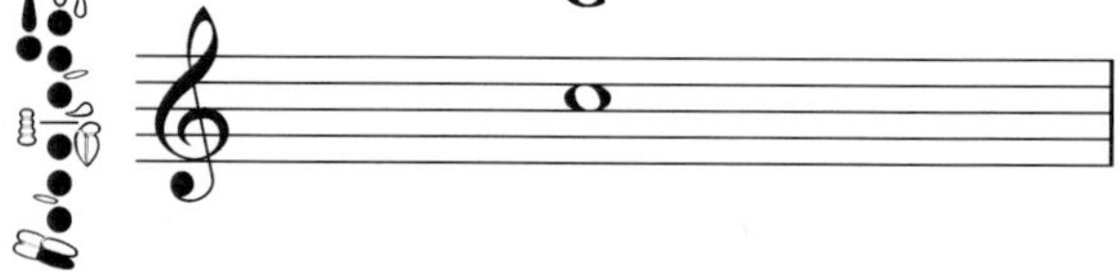

Track 20 **Bridging the Octave**

Track 21 **C major scale**

Track 22 **Over the Gap**

Track 23 **Beyond the Break**

Lesson 9

Alternate Fingerings

There are a few **alternate fingerings** that are needed to smoothly transition between certain notes. For the following six notes there are **two** different fingerings. Each note has a **left (L)** fingering and **right (R)** fingering. These names refer to which of your **pinky** fingers you will use to play the note. The following notes are grouped in pairs. The higher notes in these pairs share the same fingerings with the lower ones with the addition of the **octave key**.

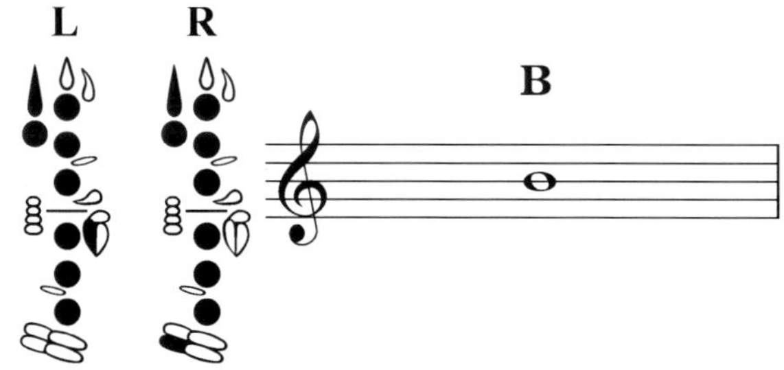

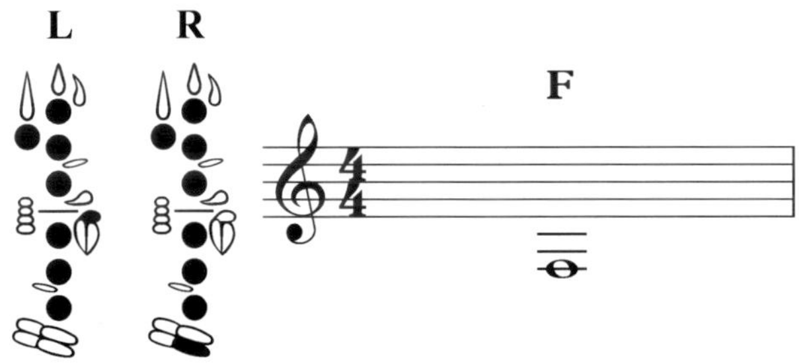

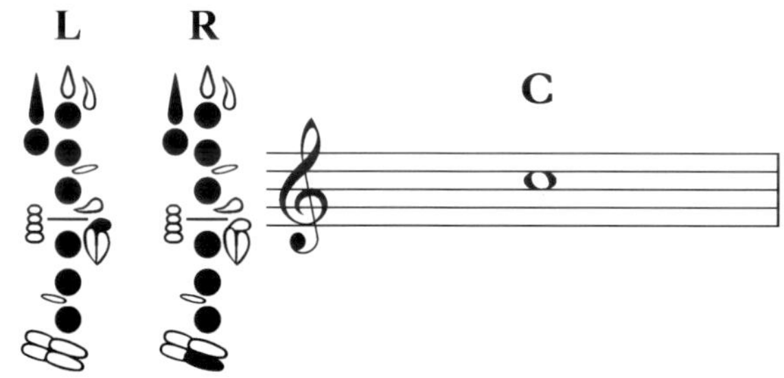

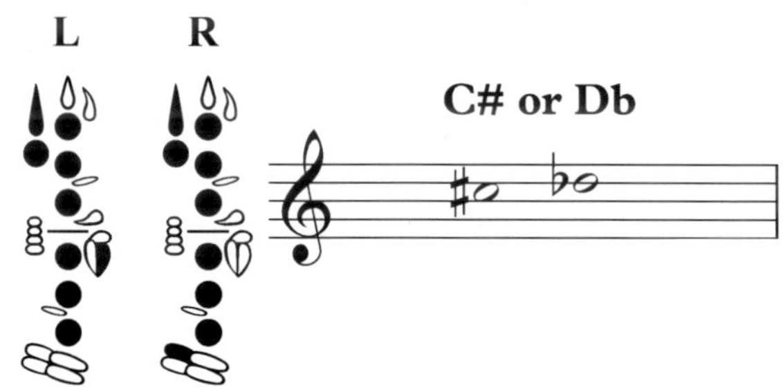

Do the following alternate fingering exercises **without** the octave key to produce the lower notes. Then **repeat** the exercises **with** the octave key to produce the higher notes.

When fingering **B** (or low **E)** on this exercise, keep down your **right** pinky that you use to play **C** (or low **F**). This way you are only moving **one** pinky (your **left** one) when moving between these notes.

When fingering **B** (or low **E)** on this exercise, keep down your **left** pinky that you use to play **C** (or low **F**). This way you are only moving **one** pinky (your **right** one) when moving between these notes.

When fingering **C#** (or low **F#)** on this exercise, keep down your **left** pinky that you use to play **B** (or low **E**). This way you are only moving **one** pinky (your **right** one) when moving between these notes.

When fingering **C#** (or low **F#)** on this exercise, keep down your **right** pinky that you use to play **B** (or low **E**). This way you are only moving **one** pinky (your **left** one) when moving between these notes.

When fingering **Db** (or low **Gb)** on this exercise, keep down your **left** pinky that you use to play **C** (or low **F**). This way you are only moving **one** pinky (your **right** one) when moving between these notes.

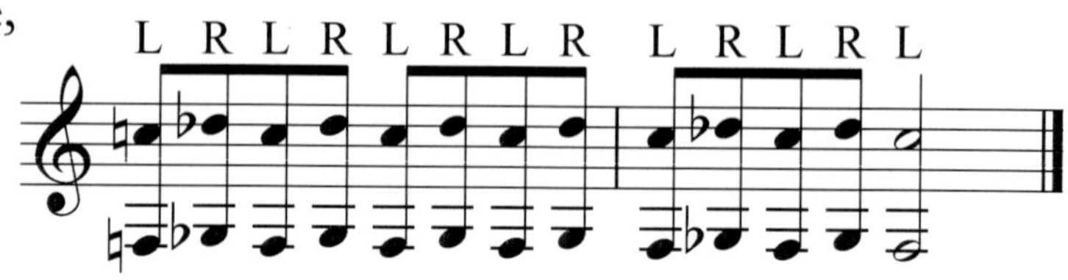

When fingering **Db** (or low **Gb)** on this exercise, keep down your **right** pinky that you use to play **C** (or low **F**). This way you are only moving **one** pinky (your **left** one) when moving between these notes.

Lesson 10

The Clarion Register

The **clarion register** is the upper range of the clarinet. This extends from the **B** we learned in **Lesson 8** to the a high **C**.

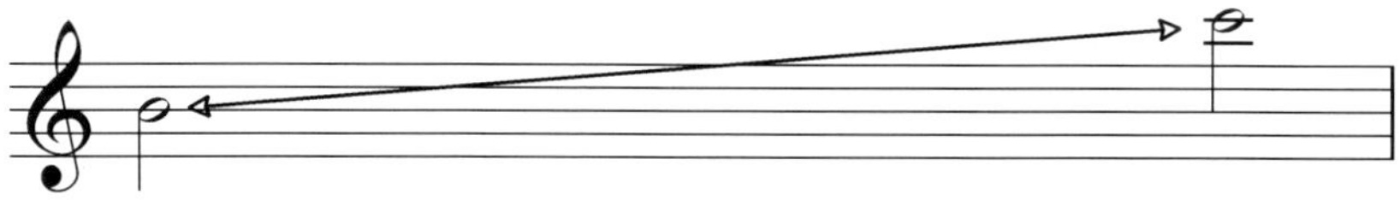

As we saw in **Lesson 9**, the first few notes that we learned in the clarion register shared the same fingerings (adding the **register** key) with lower notes that we learned in earlier lessons. The rest of the clarion register is related to the fingerings of lower notes in the same way. To achieve the **higher** notes in the following chart, use the fingering for the **lower** note and **add the register key**.

For the purposes of this book, we will only be learning notes up to the **G** above the staff. Let's take a look at the new notes we have added.

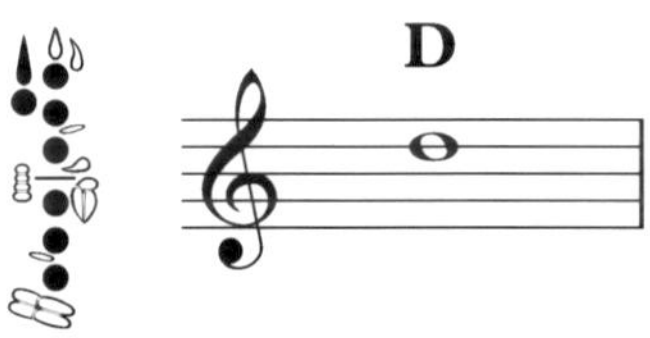

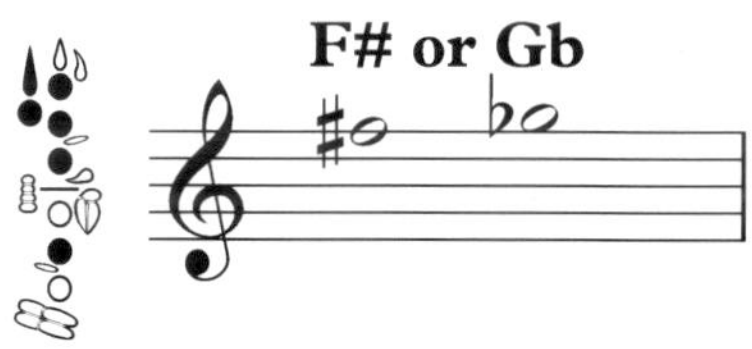

Track 24 **Exercise 10-1**

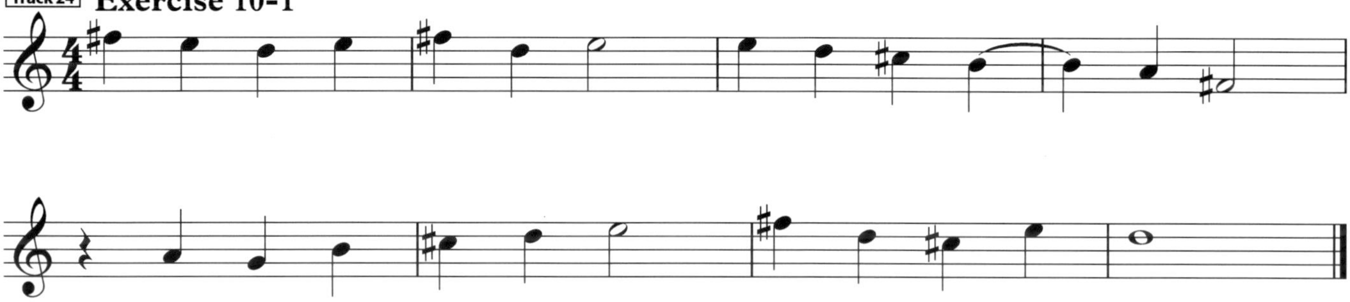

Track 25 **Exercise 10-2**

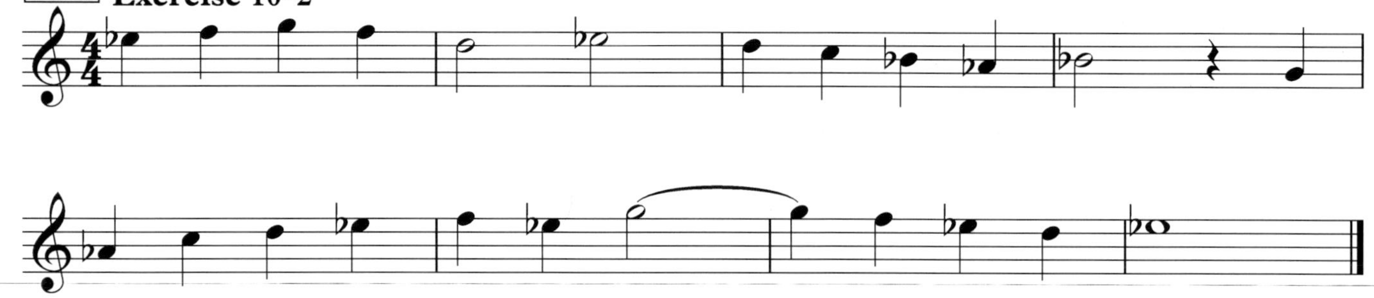

Lesson 11

Key Signatures

A **key signature** is a placed at the beginning of a piece or section and tells you what **sharps** or **flats** will be used in the piece or section. The following key signature means that all the **F**'s and **C**'s will be **sharp** in the music that follows unless noted otherwise (with a natural sign).

Now let's try the key of **Bb Major.** There are two **flats** in Bb Major - **Bb** and **Eb**. Make sure when you see a **'B'** or **'E'** that you remember to play **Bb** or **Eb** instead.

Bb Major Tune

Now let's try the key of **D Major.** There are two **sharps** in **D Major** - **F#** and **C#**.

D Major Tune

Lesson 12

Dotted Rhythms

When a **dot** is added to a note/rest, it **lengthens** that note/rest by **half** the value of that note/rest:

a **dotted half** note is 3 **quarter** notes long

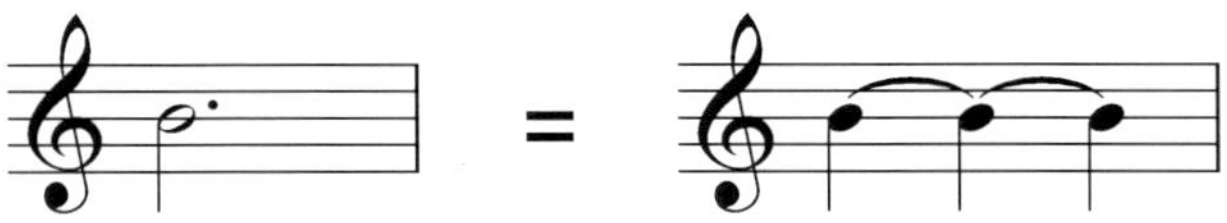

a **dotted half** rest is 3 **quarter** rests long

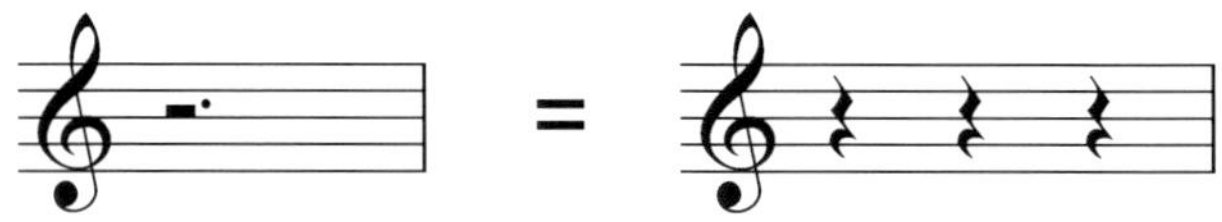

a **dotted quarter** note is 3 **eighth** notes long

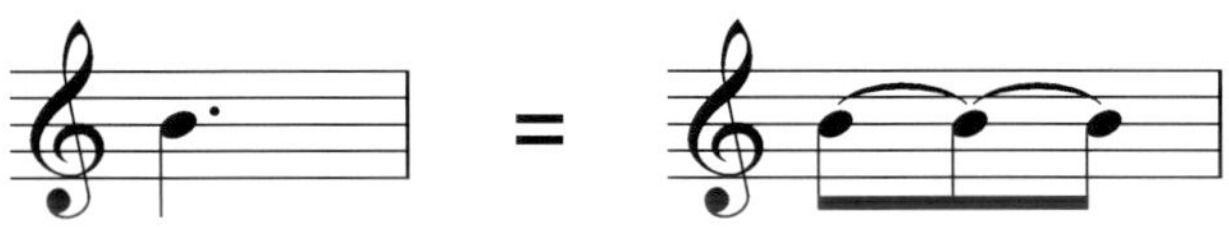

a **dotted quarter** rest is 3 **eighth** rests long

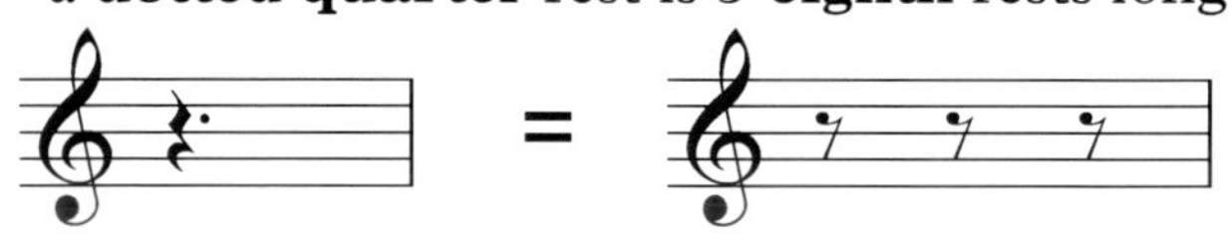

Track 28 **Lots of Dots**

Track 29 **Polka Dots**

Lesson 13

New Time Signatures: 3/4, 2/4, and 6/8

The top number of a time signature describes how many beats are in the measure. The bottom number describes what note value receives one beat. In **3/4** there are **3 beats** per measure and each beat is one **quarter** note in length. In **2/4** there are **2 beats** per measure and each beat is one **quarter** note in length. In **6/8** there are **6 beats** per measure and each beat is one **eighth** note in length.

Track 30 **Tea For Three**

Track 31 **A Few Two's**

Track 32 **A Mix of Six**

Lesson 14

Dynamics

Dynamic markings are used to indicate how soft or loud the music should be played. You can control your dynamics by adjusting how much air you use.

pp pianissimo	***p*** piano	***mp*** mezzo piano	***mf*** mezzo forte	***f*** forte	***ff*** fortissimo
very soft	soft	medium soft	medium loud	loud	very loud

Track 33 **Air Time**

Crescendos mean to play gradually louder while **decrescendos** mean to play gradually softer.

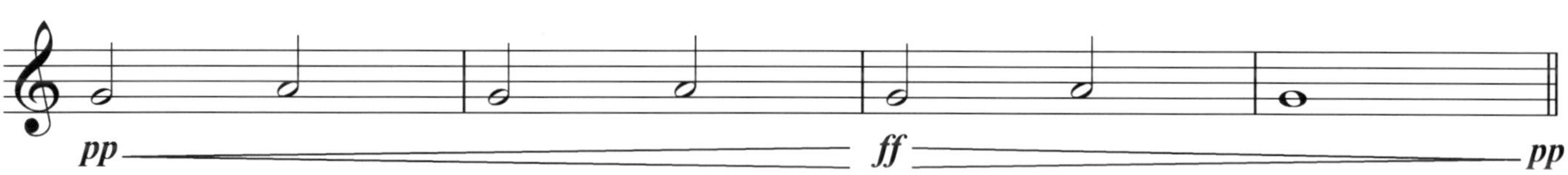

Track 34 **More or Less**

Lesson 15

Slurs

Slurs look similar to ties but instead of connecting two of the same note, a slur connects two or more different notes. Slurs are used to show a composer's intent regarding phrasing. Instead of attacking each note with your tongue, play each note in the slur with one steady breath.

Track 35 **A New Phrase**

Track 36 **Waltz in F**

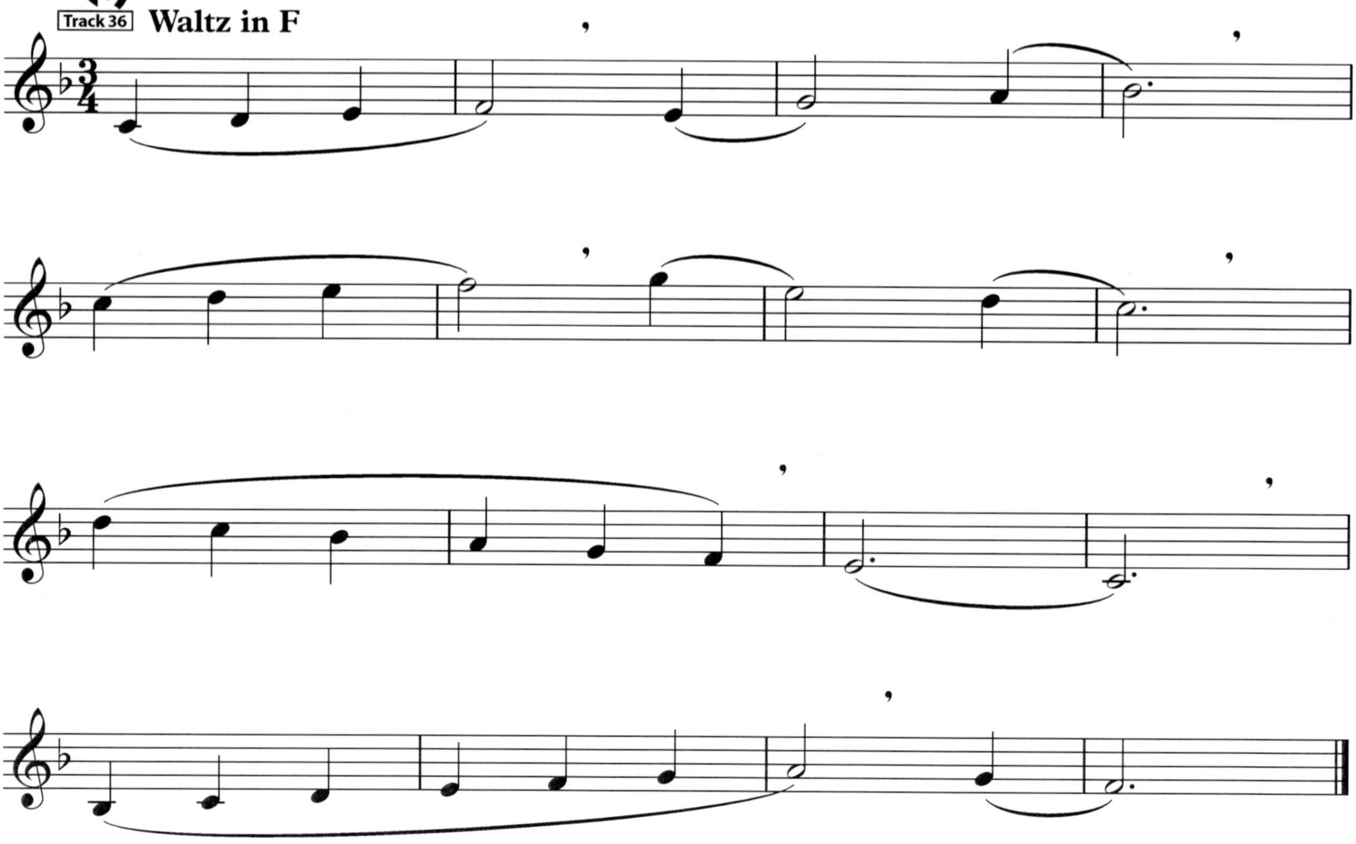

Lesson 16

Staccato

Staccato tonguing is a method of tonguing where notes are played short with gaps in between. Staccato notes are notated with a little dot above or below the notehead. To produce staccato notes, start the note with your tongue and then stop it with your tongue after the note sounds.

Staccato Exercise

Staccato Waltz

Lesson 17

Accents

Accents are used to indicate that a pitch is to be played louder than others. You can achieve the accent effect by starting the note with your tongue and using a small burst of air. Accents are notated with an **accent mark (>)** above or below the notehead.

Track 39 **The Sorcecer's Apprentice**

Paul Dukas

Track 40 **Symphony No. 5**

Ludwig van Beethoven

Lesson 18

Sixteenth Notes

Sixteenth notes are twice as fast as eighth notes. While eighth notes have one beam connecting them, sixteenth notes have two. Here are some examples of what sixteenth notes look like on their own and in groups:

Track 41 **Musette in D Major**

J.S. Bach

Lesson 19

Repeats

Repeats are used to show that a musical section should be played twice. Repeat signs come in pairs. There is a **start repeat sign** at the beginning of the musical section and an **end repeat sign** at the end. The music in between the repeat signs is played **two times**. After the second time through the section, move on to the next section.

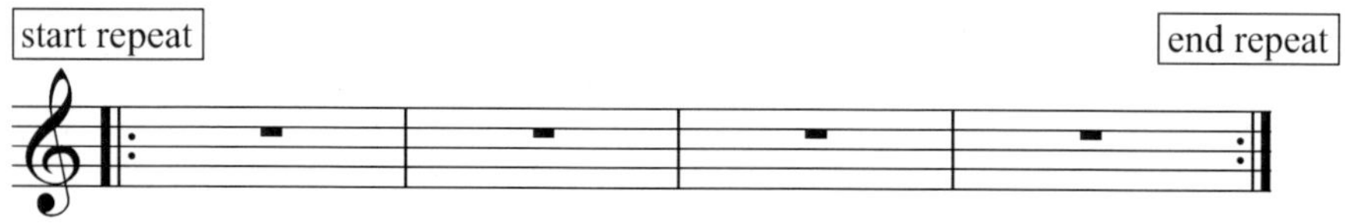

In *Minuet in G*, there are two sections. Both have repeat signs so make sure you play both sections **twice**!

Track 42 **Minuet in G**

J.S. Bach

Lesson 20

Triplets

Triplets divide the beat in to three even parts. There are two ways triplets are notated. If all three notes of an eighth note triplet are to be played then the triplet is notated with a small **3** above or below the beam of the eighth notes. If one of the notes is replaced with a rest then a bracket is drawn above or below the three notes of the triplet and a small **3** is placed in the center of that bracket.

A **triplet** means that three notes are to be played in the space of two. An eighth note triplet takes place in the space of two eighth notes (or one quarter note):

Track 43 **Triple Double**

Clarinet Fingering Chart